# John Wayne

# An American Icon

## Filiquarian Publishing, LLC.

# John Wayne

## An American Icon

John Wayne (May 26, 1907 – June 11, 1979) was an Academy Award-winning American film actor. He epitomized ruggedly individualistic masculinity, and has become an enduring American icon. He is famous for his distinctive voice, walk and enormous physical presence. He was also known for his conservative political views and his support in the 1950s for anti-communist positions.

In 1999, the American Film Institute named Wayne thirteenth among the Greatest Male Stars of All Time. A Harris Poll released in 2007 placed Wayne third among America's favorite film stars[1], the only deceased star on the list and the only one who has appeared on the poll every year.

His career began in silent movies in the 1920s and he was a major star from the 1940s to the 1970s. He is closely associated with Westerns and war movies, but he also made a wide range of films from various genres - biographies, romantic comedies, police dramas, and more.

## Early Life

Wayne was born Marion Robert Morrison[2] in Winterset, Iowa, but his name was changed to Marion Michael Morrison when his parents decided to name their next son Robert. His family was Presbyterian. His father, Clyde Leonard Morrison (1884-1937), was of Irish and Scots-Irish [3] and English descent [4], and the son of American Civil War veteran Marion Mitchell Morrison (20 January 1845-05 December 1915). Marion Mitchell was born in Cherry Fork, Adams, Ohio as the son of Robert Morrison and Mary Mitchell. Wayne's mother, Mary Alberta Brown, was also of Irish descent.[5]

Wayne's family moved to Palmdale, California, and then to Glendale, California in 1911, where his father worked as a pharmacist in a drug store. A local fireman at the firehouse on his route to school in Glendale started calling him "Little Duke", because he never went anywhere without his huge Airedale Terrier dog, Duke.[6][7] He preferred "Duke" to "Marion", and the name stuck for the rest of his life.

As a teen, Wayne worked in an ice cream shop for a person who shoed horses for local Hollywood studios. He was also active as a member of the Order of DeMolay, a youth organization associated with the Freemasons, that he joined when he came of age. He attended Wilson Middle School in Glendale. He played football for the 1924 champion Glendale High School team.

Wayne applied to the U.S. Naval Academy, but was not accepted. He instead attended the University of Southern California (USC), majoring in pre-law. He was a member of the Trojan Knights and joined the Sigma Chi fraternity. Wayne also played on the USC football team under legendary coach Howard Jones. An injury curtailed his athletic career; Wayne later noted he was too terrified of Jones' reaction to reveal the actual cause of his injury, which was bodysurfing at the "Wedge" at the tip of the Balboa Peninsula in Newport Beach. He lost his athletic scholarship and without funds had to leave school.[8]

While at the university, Wayne began working at the local film studios. Western star Tom Mix got him a summer job in the prop department in exchange for football tickets, and Wayne soon moved on to bit parts, establishing a long friendship with director John Ford, who provided most of those bit parts. Early in this period, Wayne appeared with his USC teammates playing on-screen football in The Dropkick, Brown of Harvard, and Salute, and was one of the featured football players in Columbia Pictures' Maker of Men (filmed in 1930 and released in 1931).[9]

## Film Career

After two years working as a prop man at the Fox Film Corporation for $75 a week, his first starring role was in the 1930 movie The Big Trail. The first western epic sound motion picture established his screen credentials, although it was a commercial failure. Before this film, Wayne had only been given on-screen credit once (in Words and Music), as "Duke Morrison". The director Raoul Walsh, who "discovered" Wayne, suggested giving him the stage name "Anthony Wayne", after Revolutionary War general "Mad Anthony" Wayne. Fox Studios chief Winfield Sheehan rejected "Anthony Wayne" as sounding "too Italian." Walsh then suggested "John Wayne." Sheehan agreed and the name was set. Wayne himself was not even present for the discussion.[10] His pay was raised to $105 a week.

Wayne continued making westerns, most notably at Monogram Pictures, and serials for Mascot Pictures Corporation, including The Three Musketeers (1933), a French Foreign Legion tale with no resemblance to the novel which inspired its title. Coincidentally, he also appeared in some of the Three Mesquiteers westerns whose title was a play on the Alexandre Dumas, père classic. He was tutored by stuntmen in riding and other western skills.[11] He and famed stuntman Yakima Canutt developed and perfected stunts still used today.

Beginning in 1928 and extending over the next 35 years, Wayne appeared in more than twenty of John Ford's films, including Stagecoach (1939), She Wore a Yellow Ribbon (1949), The Quiet Man (1952), The Searchers (1956), The Wings of Eagles (1957), and The Man Who Shot Liberty Valance (1962). His performance in Stagecoach made him a star.

His first color film was Shepherd of the Hills (1941), in which he co-starred with his longtime friend Harry Carey. The following year he appeared in his only film directed by Cecil B. DeMille, the Technicolor epic Reap the Wild Wind, in which he co-starred with Ray Milland and Paulette Goddard; it was one of the rare times he played a character with questionable values.

In 1949, director Robert Rossen offered the starring role of All the King's Men to Wayne. Wayne refused, believing the script to be un-American in many ways. Broderick Crawford, who eventually got the role, won the 1949 Oscar for best male actor, ironically beating out Wayne, who had been nominated for Sands of Iwo Jima.

He lost the leading role in The Gunfighter to
Gregory Peck because of his refusal to work for
Columbia Pictures after Columbia chief Harry
Cohn had mistreated him years before as a young
contract player. Cohn had bought the project for
Wayne, but Wayne's grudge was too deep, and
Cohn sold the script to Twentieth Century Fox,
which cast Peck in the role Wayne badly wanted
but refused to bend for.

One of Wayne's most popular roles was in The
High and the Mighty (1954), directed by William
Wellman and based on a novel by Ernest K. Gann.
His portrayal of a heroic airman won widespread
acclaim.

The Searchers continues to be widely regarded as
perhaps Wayne's finest and most complex
performance. In 2006 Premiere Magazine ran an
industry poll in which his portrayal of Ethan
Edwards was rated the 87th greatest performance
in film history. He named his youngest son Ethan
after the character.

John Wayne won a Best Actor Oscar for True Grit
(1969). Wayne was also nominated as the
producer of Best Picture for The Alamo, one of
two films he directed. The other was The Green
Berets (1968), the only major film made during
the Vietnam War to support the war.[12] During
the filming of Green Berets, the Degar or
Montagnard people of Vietnam's Central
Highlands, fierce fighters against communism,
bestowed on Wayne a brass bracelet that he wore
in the film and all subsequent films.

According to the Internet Movie Database, Wayne
played the lead in 142 of his film appearances.

Batjac, the production company co-founded by
Wayne, was named after the fictional shipping
company Batjak in Wake of the Red Witch. (A
spelling error by Wayne's secretary was allowed to
stand, accounting for the variation.) Batjac (and its
predecessor, Wayne-Fellows Productions) was the
arm through which Wayne produced many films
for himself and other stars. Its best-known non-
Wayne production was the highly acclaimed
Seven Men from Now, which started the classic

collaboration between director Budd Boetticher and star Randolph Scott.

In later years, Wayne was recognized as a sort of American natural resource, and his various critics, political and film, looked on him with more respect. Abbie Hoffman, the radical of the 1960's, paid tribute to Wayne's singularity. Reviewing The Cowboys, made in 1972, Vincent Canby, film critic of the New York Times, who did not particularly care for the film, wrote, "Wayne is, of course, marvelously indestructible, and he has become an almost perfect father figure." But years before he became anything close to a father figure, Wayne had become a symbolic male figure, a man of impregnable virility and the embodiment of simplistic, laconic virtues, packaged in a well-built 6-foot-4-inch, 225- pound frame (1.94 m, 102 kg). (His height has been disputed.)

He had a handsome and hearty face, with crinkles around eyes that gave the impression of a man of action, an outdoor man who chafed at a settled life. He was laconic on screen. And when he shambled into view, audiences sensed the arrival of coiled vigor awaiting only provocation to be sprung. His demeanor and his roles were those of a man who did not look for trouble but was relentless in tackling it when it affronted him. This screen presence emerged particularly under the ministrations of directors John Ford and Howard Hawks.

## 1964 Illness

In 1964, Wayne was diagnosed with lung cancer, and underwent successful surgery to remove his entire left lung and four ribs. Despite efforts by his business associates to prevent him from going public with his illness (for fear it would cost him work), Wayne announced he had cancer and called on the public to get preventive examinations. Five years later, Wayne was declared cancer-free. Despite the fact that Wayne's diminished lung capacity left him incapable of prolonged exertion and frequently in need of supplemental oxygen, within a few years of his operation he chewed tobacco and began smoking cigars.

# Politics

Wayne was politically a conservative Republican. He took part in creating the Motion Picture Alliance for the Preservation of American Ideals in 1943 and was elected president of that organization in 1947. He was an ardent anti-communist and vocal supporter of the House Un-American Activities Committee. In 1951, he made Big Jim McLain to show his support for the anti-communist cause. He also claimed to have been instrumental in having Carl Foreman blacklisted from Hollywood after the release of the anti-McCarthyism western High Noon, and later teamed up with Howard Hawks to make Rio Bravo as a right-wing response. Wayne used his iconic status to support conservative causes, including rallying support for the Vietnam War by producing, co-directing, and starring in the critically panned The Green Berets (1968). In 1978 however, he enraged conservatives by supporting liberal causes such as the Panama Canal Treaty[13] and the innocence of Patty Hearst.[14]

Due to his enormous popularity, and his status as the most famous Republican star in Hollywood, wealthy Texas Republican Party backers asked Wayne to run for national office in 1968, as had his friend and fellow actor, Senator George Murphy. He declined, joking that he did not believe the public would seriously consider an actor in the White House. However, he did support his friend Ronald Reagan's runs for Governor of California in 1966 and 1970. He was also asked to be the running mate for Democratic Alabama Governor George Wallace in 1968. Wayne vehemently rejected the offer.[15] Wayne actively campaigned for Richard Nixon[16], and addressed the Republican National Convention on its opening day in August 1968. Wayne also was a member of the conservative and anti-communist John Birch Society.[17]

Wayne's strong anti-communist politics led to a particularly unnerving situation. Information from Soviet archives, reported in 2003, indicates that Joseph Stalin ordered Wayne's assassination, but died before the killing could be accomplished. His successor, Khrushchev, reportedly told Wayne during a 1958 visit to the United States that he had personally rescinded the order.[18][19]

In an interview with Playboy magazine in May 1971, Wayne made infamous remarks. One disclaimed a personal sense of guilt for the historical treatment of Native Americans, the second claimed that African-Americans had been denied educational opportunities and resented that fact, "possibly rightfully so." He went on to say that did not justify turning over the country "to the leadership of the blacks. I believe in white supremacy until the blacks are educated to a point of responsibility. I don't believe in giving authority and positions of leadership and judgment to irresponsible people."[20]

## Military Service Controversy

America's entrance into World War II resulted in a deluge of support for the war effort from all sectors of society, and Hollywood was no exception. Established stars such as Douglas Fairbanks, Jr. (USN, Silver Star), Henry Fonda (USN, Bronze Star), and Clark Gable (USAAC) as well as emerging actors such as Eddie Albert

(USN, Bronze Star) and Tyrone Power (USMC) rushed to sign up for military service. As the majority of male leads left Hollywood to serve overseas, John Wayne saw his just-beginning stardom at risk. Despite enormous pressure from his inner circle of friends, he put off enlisting. Wayne was exempted from service due to his age (34 at the time of Pearl Harbor) and family status, classified as 3-A (family deferment). Wayne's secretary recalled making inquiries of military officials on behalf of his interest in enlisting, "but he never really followed up on them."[21] He repeatedly wrote to John Ford, asking to be placed in Ford's military unit, but continually postponed it until "after he finished one more film."[22] Republic Studios was emphatically resistant to losing Wayne, especially after the loss of Gene Autry to the army.[23] Correspondence between Wayne and Herbert J. Yates (the head of Republic) indicates that Yates threatened Wayne with a lawsuit if he walked away from his contract, though the likelihood of a studio suing its biggest star for going to war was minute.[24] The threat was real, but whether Wayne took it seriously or not, he did not test it. Selective Service Records indicate he did not attempt to prevent his reclassification as 1-A (draft eligible), but apparently Republic Pictures intervened directly, requesting his further deferment.[25] In May, 1944, Wayne was reclassified as 1-A (draft eligible), but the studio obtained another 2-A deferment (for "support of national health, safety, or interest").[26] He remained 2-A until the war's end. John Wayne did not "dodge" the draft, but he never took direct positive action toward enlistment. Wayne was in the South Pacific theatre of the war for three months in 1943-'44, touring U.S. bases and hospitals as well as doing some "undercover" work for OSS commander William J. "Wild Bill" Donovan, who thought Wayne's celebrity might be good cover for an assessment of the causes for poor relations between General Douglas MacArthur and Donovan's OSS Pacific network. Wayne filed a report and Donovan gave him a plaque and commendation for serving with the OSS, but Wayne dismissed it as meaningless.[27]

The foregoing facts influenced the direction of Wayne's later life. By all accounts, Wayne's failure to serve in the military during World War II was the most painful experience of his life.[28]

There were some other stars who, for various reasons, did not enlist. But Wayne, by virtue of becoming a celluloid war hero in several patriotic war films, as well as an outspoken supporter of right-wing political causes and the Vietnam War, became the focus of particular disdain from both himself and certain portions of the public, particularly in later years. While some hold Wayne in contempt for the paradox between his early actions and his later attitudes, his widow suggests that Wayne's rampant patriotism in later decades sprang not from hypocrisy but from guilt. Pilar Wayne wrote, "He would become a 'superpatriot' for the rest of his life trying to atone for staying home."[29]

## Personal Life

Wayne was married three times and divorced twice. His wives, all of them Hispanic women, were Josephine Alicia Saenz, Esperanza Baur, and Pilar Pallete. He had four children with Josephine and three with Pilar, including the producer Michael Wayne and actor Patrick Wayne. Wayne is also the great-uncle of boxing heavyweight Tommy Morrison.[30] Wayne's son Ethan was billed as John Ethan Wayne in a few films and played one of the leads in the 90's update of the Adam-12 television series.

John Wayne's hair began thinning in the 1940s and he began wearing a hairpiece by the end of that decade (though his receding hairline is quite evident in Rio Grande). He was occasionally seen in public without the hairpiece (notably, according to Life Magazine photos, at Gary Cooper's funeral). The only time he unintentionally appeared on film without it was for a split second in North to Alaska. On the first punch of the climactic fistfight, Wayne's hat flies off, revealing a brief flash of his unadorned scalp. Wayne also has several scenes in The Wings of Eagles where he is without his hairpiece.

Wayne had several high-profile affairs, including one with Marlene Dietrich that lasted for three years.[31] In the years prior to his death, Wayne was romantically involved with his former secretary Pat Stacy (1941-1995).[32] She wrote a biography of her life with him, DUKE: A Love Story (1983).

During the early 1960s John Wayne traveled extensively to Panama. During this time, the actor reportedly purchased the island of Taborcillo off the main coast of Panama. It was sold by his estate at his death and changed hands many times before being opened as a tourist attraction.

## Death

John Wayne died of stomach cancer on June 11, 1979, at the UCLA Medical Center, and was interred in the Pacific View Memorial Park cemetery in Corona del Mar. According to his son Patrick, he converted to Roman Catholicism shortly before his death.[33] He requested his tombstone read "Feo, Fuerte y Formal", a Spanish epitaph meaning "ugly, strong and serious".[34] However, the grave, unmarked for twenty years, is now marked with a quotation from his controversial 1971 Playboy interview: "Tomorrow is the most important thing in life. Comes into us at midnight very clean. It's perfect when it arrives and it puts itself in our hands. It hopes we've learned something from yesterday."

A relatively large number of the cast and crew of Wayne's 1956 film The Conqueror developed various forms of cancer. The film was shot in Southwestern Utah, east and generally downwind of where the U.S. Government had tested nuclear weapons in Southeastern Nevada, and many contend that radioactive fallout from these tests contaminated the film location and the film crew working there. Despite the suggestion that Wayne's 1964 lung cancer and his 1979 stomach cancer resulted from this nuclear contamination, he himself believed his lung cancer to have been a result of his five-pack-a-day cigarette habit.[35] The effect of nuclear fallout on The Conqueror's cast and crew, and particularly on Wayne, is the subject of James Morrow's science-fiction short story Martyrs of the Upshot Knothole.[36]

## Congressional Gold Medal and Presidential Medal of Freedom

John Wayne's enduring status as an iconic American was formally recognized by the United States Congress on May 26, 1979 when he was awarded the Congressional Gold Medal.[37][38] Hollywood figures and American leaders from

across the political spectrum, including Elizabeth
Taylor, Frank Sinatra, Mike Frankovich,
Katharine Hepburn, General and Mrs. Omar
Bradley, Gregory Peck, Robert Stack, James
Arness, and Kirk Douglas, testified to Congress of
the merit and deservedness of this award, most
notably Robert Aldrich, then president of the
Directors Guild of America, who stated, "It is
important for you to know that I am a registered
Democrat and, to my knowledge, share none of
the political views espoused by Duke. However,
whether he is ill disposed or healthy, John Wayne
is far beyond the normal political sharp shooting
in this community. Because of his courage, his
dignity, his integrity, and because of his talents as
an actor, his strength as a leader, his warmth as a
human being throughout his illustrious career, he
is entitled to a unique spot in our hearts and
minds. In this industry, we often judge people,
sometimes unfairly, by asking whether they have
paid their dues. John Wayne has paid his dues
over and over, and I'm proud to consider him a
friend, and am very much in favor of my
Government recognizing in some important
fashion the contribution that Mr. Wayne has
made." Maureen O'Hara, Wayne's close friend,

initiated the petition for the medal and requested the words that would be placed onto the medal: "It is my great honor to be here. I beg you to strike a medal for Duke, to order the President to strike it. And I feel that the medal should say just one thing, 'John Wayne, American.'"[39] The medal crafted by the United States Mint has on one side John Wayne riding on horseback, and the other side has a portrait of Wayne with the words, "John Wayne, American." This Congressional Gold Medal was presented to the family of John Wayne in a ceremony held on March 6, 1980 at the United States Capitol. This medal is now at the John Wayne Museum in Winterset, Iowa. Copies were made and sold in large numbers to the public.

On June 9, 1980, Wayne was posthumously awarded the Presidential Medal of Freedom by Jimmy Carter (at whose inaugural ball Wayne had appeared "as a member of the loyal opposition", as Wayne described it in his speech to the gathering). Thus Wayne received the two highest civilian decorations awarded by the United States government.

## American Icon

John Wayne rose beyond the typical recognition for a famous actor to that of an enduring icon who symbolized and communicated American values and ideals. By the middle of his career, Wayne had developed a larger-than-life image, and as his career progressed, he selected roles that would not compromise his off-screen image. By the time of his last film The Shootist (1976), Wayne refused to allow his character to shoot a man in the back as was originally scripted. [40]

Wayne's rise to being the quintessential movie war hero began to take shape four years after World War II when Sands of Iwo Jima (1949) was released. His footprints at Grauman's Chinese theater in Hollywood were laid in cement that contained sand from Iwo Jima.[41] His status grew so large and legendary that when Japanese Emperor Hirohito visited the United States in 1975, he asked to meet John Wayne, the symbolic representation of his country's former enemy.

Wayne was a popular visitor to the war zones in World War II, Korea, and Vietnam. By the 1950s, perhaps in large part due to the military aspect of films such as the Sands of Iwo Jima, Flying Tigers, They Were Expendable, and the Ford cavalry trilogy, Wayne had become an icon to all the branches of the U.S. Military, even in light of his actual lack of military service. Many veterans have said their reason for serving was in some part related to watching Wayne's movies. His name is attached to various pieces of gear, such as the P-38 "John Wayne" can-opener, so named because "it can do anything", paper towels known as "John Wayne Toilet Paper" because "it's rough and it's tough and don't take shit off no one", and C-Ration crackers are called "John Wayne crackers" because presumably only someone as tough as Wayne could eat them.

Various public locations have been named in memory of John Wayne. They include John Wayne Airport in Orange County, California, where his life-size statue graces the entrance; the John Wayne Marina near Sequim, Washington; John Wayne Elementary School (P.S. 380) in Brooklyn, NY, which boasts a 38 foot mosaic mural commission by New York artist Knox Martin[42] entitled "John Wayne and the

American Frontier"; and a 100-plus mile trail named the "John Wayne Pioneer Trail" in Washington state's Iron Horse State Park. A larger than life-size bronze statue of Wayne atop a horse was erected at the corner of La Cienega Blvd. and Wilshire Blvd. in Beverly Hills, California at the former offices of the Great Western Savings & Loan Corporation, for whom Wayne had done a number of commercials. (The building now houses Larry Flynt Enterprises.)

On December 5, 2007, California Governor Arnold Schwarzenegger and First Lady Maria Shriver inducted Wayne into the California Hall of Fame, located at The California Museum for History, Women and the Arts.[43]

## Celebrations and Landmarks

Several celebrations took place on May 26, 2007, the centenary of John Wayne's birth.

In his birthplace of Winterset, Iowa, the John Wayne Birthday Centennial Celebration was held on May 25-27, 2007. The celebration included chuckwagon suppers, concerts by Michael Martin

Murphey and Riders in the Sky, a Wild West Revue in the style of Buffalo Bill's Wild West show, symposia with John Wayne co-stars, cavalry and trick horse demonstrations as well as many of John Wayne's films. This event also included the groundbreaking for the John Wayne Museum and Learning Center at his birthplace house.

In 2006, friends of Wayne's and his Arizona business partner, Louis Johnson inaugurated the first annual "Louie and the Duke Classics"[3] events benefiting the John Wayne Cancer Foundation[4] and the American Cancer Society. The weekend long event each fall in Casa Grande includes a golf tournament, an auction of John Wayne memorabilia and a team roping competition."

## Missed Roles

* John Wayne desperately wanted the role of "Jimmy Ringo" in the 1950 film The Gunfighter directed by Henry King[44] but the role instead went to Gregory Peck. John Wayne's final film,

The Shootist (1976)[45] directed by Don Siegel was very similar to The Gunfighter.

* An urban legend has it that John Wayne was offered the leading role of Matt Dillon in the longtime favorite television show Gunsmoke, but he turned it down, recommending instead James Arness for the role. The only part of this story that is true is that Wayne did indeed recommend Arness for the part. Wayne introduced Arness in a prologue to the first episode of Gunsmoke. [46]

* Wayne was approached by Mel Brooks to play the part of The Waco Kid in the film Blazing Saddles. After reading the script he said, "I can't be in this picture, it's too dirty...but I'll be the first in line to see it."[47]

* Wayne reportedly refused the role that Lee Marvin played in The Dirty Dozen and chose instead the part in the The Green Berets.[48]

* He also turned down the title role in Dirty Harry, although the film's director Don Siegel said Wayne would have been too old to play the part anyway. Wayne later made two cop movies of his

own, McQ and Brannigan, which were not particularly successful.

* Another role that Wayne missed was the title role in the film Patton (1970). George C. Scott took the role instead.

* According to his autobiography Kiss Me Like A Stranger, Gene Wilder states that he wanted to work with Wayne for the upcoming film The Frisco Kid. Wayne loved the script, especially Wilder's "little rabbi character", but when the producers tried to get him to accept $750,000 instead of his $1,000,000 fee, he backed out. Harrison Ford played the role intended for him instead.

## Famous Movie Quotes

* "I won't be wronged, I won't be insulted, and I won't be laid a hand on. I don't do these things to other people, and I require the same from them." (The Shootist)

\* Speaking to his young cavalry lieutenants: "Don't apologize—it's a sign of weakness." (She Wore a Yellow Ribbon)

\* "Fill your hands, you sonofabitch!" (True Grit)

\* "That'll be the day!" (The Searchers - Spoken several times; inspired Buddy Holly to write a song with that title.)

\* "Pilgrim." (The Man Who Shot Liberty Valance - Reportedly he used the expression "Pilgrim", as in "tenderfoot" or "dude" or "amateur", 23 times in that film, and once also in McLintock!. It became a catchphrase for impressionists such as John Byner, and Rich Little)

\* "I haven't lost my temper in 40 years; but, Pilgrim, you caused a lot of trouble this morning; might have got somebody killed; and somebody oughta belt you in the mouth. But I won't. I won't. The hell I won't!" (He belts him). (To Leo Gordon in McLintock!).

\* "You can call me Dad, you can call me Father, you can call me Jacob and you can call me Jake.

**John Wayne**

You can call me a dirty old son-of-a-bitch, but if you EVER call me Daddy again, I'll finish this fight." (To his son, played by his real-life son Patrick Wayne, in Big Jake).

# An American Icon

# Notes and Sources

1. Harris Interactive | The Harris Poll - Denzel Washington: America's Favorite Movie Star

2. Madison Co., Iowa birth certificate

3. John Wayne's grave

4. http://wc.rootsweb.com/

5. John Wayne's grave

6. Roberts, Randy, and James S. Olson. John Wayne: American. New York: Free Press, 1995 ISBN 978-0029238370, p. 37

7. Munn, Michael. John Wayne: The Man Behind the Myth. London: Robson Books, 2003 ISBN 0-451-21244-4, p. 7

8. jwayne.com

9. library.thinkquest.org article

10. Roberts & Olson, p. 84

11. thinkquest.org article

12. jwayne.com

13. Time Magazine, October 31, 1977

14. Slate Magazine, January 28, 2002

15. Jim Beaver, "John Wayne". Films in Review, Volume 28, Number 5, May 1977, pp. 265-284

16. Judis, John, "Kevin Phillips, Ex-Populist: Elite Model," The New Republic, May 22, 2006

17. John Wayne, Man and Myth, The Washington Post, September 25, 1995

18. Montefiore, Sebag, Stalin: The Court of the Red Tsar, London: George Weidenfeld & Nicholson, 2003

19. " Why Stalin loved Tarzan and wanted John Wayne shot." Daily Telegraph. 6 April 2004. [2]

20. Playboy, May, 1972

21. Roberts & Olson, John Wayne: American, p. 211

22. Roberts & Olson, John Wayne: American, p. 212

23. Gene Autry, who was also Wayne's age, gave an interview in 1942 that seemed to later biographers to chastise Wayne for his refusal to enlist and provide an example for younger actors in Hollywood: "I think the He-men in the movies belong in the Army, Marine, Navy or Air Corps. All of these He-men in the movies realize that right now is the time to get into the service. Every movie cowboy ought to devote time to the Army winning, or to helping win, until the war is over - the same as any other American citizen. The Army needs all the young men it can get, and if I can set a good example for the young men I'll be mighty proud." Source: Wills, Gary, John Wayne's America, pp. 221-223

24. Roberts & Olson, p. 220

25. Roberts & Olson, p. 213

26. Roberts & Olson, p. 213

27. Roberts & Olson, p. 253

28. Roberts & Olson, p. 212

29. Wayne, Pilar, John Wayne, pp. 43-47

30. The Great White Hope climbs back between the ropes

31. Olson & Roberts, John Wayne: American, pp. 195-197

32. jwayne.com

33. The religion of John Wayne, actor

34. Candelaria, Nash. John Wayne, Person and Personal The love affairs of an American legend in Hopscotch: A Cultural Review - Volume 2, Number 4, 2001, pp. 2-13, Duke University Press

35. Article Archive

36. Morrow, James. In The Cat's Pajamas and Other Stories, Tachyon Publications, 2004. ISBN 1892391155

37. http://en.wikipedia.org/wiki/ListofCongressionalG oldMedalrecipients

38. John Wayne's Congressional Gold Medal

39. Hearing Before the Subcommittee on Consumer Affairs of the Committee on Banking, Finance and Urban Affairs, House of Representatives, 96th Congress, First Session, on H.R. 3767, A Bill to Authorize the President of the United States to Present on Behalf of the Congress a Specially Struck Gold Medal to John Wayne, May 21, 1979, Serial 96-10

40. The Shootist (1976) - Trivia

41. Endres, Stacey and Robert Cushman. Hollywood At Your Feet. Beverly Hills: Pomegranate Press, 1993 ISBN 0-938817-08-6

42. Knox Martin - Home

43. Wayne inducted into California Hall of Fame, California Museum, Accessed 2007

44. http://www.imdb.com/title/tt0042531/

45. http://www.imdb.com/title/tt0075213/

46. http://www.snopes.com/radiotv/tv/gunsmok2.htm

47. Interview with Mel Brooks on DVD release of Blazing Saddles

48. washingtonpost.com

## Further Reading

* Roberts, Randy, and James S. Olson. John Wayne: American. New York: Free Press, 1995 ISBN 978-0029238370

* Campbell, James T. "Print the Legend: John Wayne and Postwar American Culture". Reviews

in American History, Volume 28, Number 3, September 2000, pp. 465-477

* Shepherd, Donald, and Robert Slatzer, with Dave Grayson. Duke: The Life and Times of John Wayne. New York: Doubleday, 1985 ISBN 0-385-17893-X

* Carey, Harry Jr. A Company of Heroes: My Life as an Actor in the John Ford Stock Company. Lanham, Maryland: Scarecrow Press, 1994 ISBN 0-8108-2865-0

* Clark, Donald & Christopher Anderson. John Wayne's The Alamo: The Making of the Epic Film. New York: Carol Publishing Group, 1995 ISBN 0-8065-1625-9 (pbk.)

* Eyman, Scott. Print the Legend: The Life and Times of John Ford. New York: Simon & Schuster, 1999 ISBN 0-684-81161-8

* McCarthy, Todd. Howard Hawks: The Grey Fox of Hollywood. New York: Grove Press, 1997 ISBN 0-8021-1598-5

* Maurice Zolotow., Shooting Star: A Biography of John Wayne. New York: Simon & Schuster, 1974 ISBN 0671829696

* Jim Beaver, "John Wayne". Films in Review, Volume 28, Number 5, May 1977, pp. 265-284.

* McGivern, Carolyn. John Wayne: A Giant Shadow. Bracknell, England: Sammon, 2000 ISBN 0-9540031-0-1

* Munn, Michael. John Wayne: The Man Behind the Myth. London: Robson Books, 2003 ISBN 0-451-21244-4

**John Wayne**

# GNU Free Documentation License

Version 1.2, November 2002

## 0. PREAMBLE

The purpose of this License is to make a manual, textbook, or other functional and useful document "free" in the sense of freedom: to assure everyone the effective freedom to copy and redistribute it, with or without modifying it, either commercially or noncommercially. Secondarily, this License preserves for the author and publisher a way to get credit for their work, while not being considered responsible for modifications made by others.

This License is a kind of "copyleft", which means that derivative works of the document must themselves be free in the same sense. It complements the GNU General Public License, which is a copyleft license designed for free software.

We have designed this License in order to use it for manuals for free software, because free software needs free documentation: a free program should come with manuals providing the same freedoms that the software does. But this License is not limited to software manuals; it can be used for any textual work, regardless of subject matter or whether it is published as a printed book. We recommend this License principally for works whose purpose is instruction or reference.

**An American Icon**

## 1. APPLICABILITY AND DEFINITIONS

This License applies to any manual or other work, in any medium, that contains a notice placed by the copyright holder saying it can be distributed under the terms of this License. Such a notice grants a world-wide, royalty-free license, unlimited in duration, to use that work under the conditions stated herein. The "Document", below, refers to any such manual or work. Any member of the public is a licensee, and is addressed as "you". You accept the license if you copy, modify or distribute the work in a way requiring permission under copyright law.

A "Modified Version" of the Document means any work containing the Document or a portion of it, either copied verbatim, or with modifications and/or translated into another language.

A "Secondary Section" is a named appendix or a front-matter section of the Document that deals exclusively with the relationship of the publishers or authors of the Document to the Document's overall subject (or to related matters) and contains nothing that could fall directly within that overall subject. (Thus, if the Document is in part a textbook of mathematics, a Secondary Section may not explain any mathematics.) The relationship could be a matter of historical connection with the subject or with related matters, or of legal, commercial, philosophical, ethical or political position regarding them.

The "Invariant Sections" are certain Secondary Sections whose titles are designated, as being those of Invariant Sections, in the notice that says that the Document is released under this License. If a section does not fit the above definition of Secondary then it is not allowed to be designated as Invariant. The Document may contain zero Invariant Sections. If the Document does not identify any Invariant Sections then there are none.

The "Cover Texts" are certain short passages of text that are listed, as Front-Cover Texts or Back-Cover Texts, in the notice that says that the Document is released under this License. A Front-Cover Text may be at most 5 words, and a Back-Cover Text may be at most 25 words.

## John Wayne

A "Transparent" copy of the Document means a machine-readable copy, represented in a format whose specification is available to the general public, that is suitable for revising the document straightforwardly with generic text editors or (for images composed of pixels) generic paint programs or (for drawings) some widely available drawing editor, and that is suitable for input to text formatters or for automatic translation to a variety of formats suitable for input to text formatters. A copy made in an otherwise Transparent file format whose markup, or absence of markup, has been arranged to thwart or discourage subsequent modification by readers is not Transparent. An image format is not Transparent if used for any substantial amount of text. A copy that is not "Transparent" is called "Opaque".

Examples of suitable formats for Transparent copies include plain ASCII without markup, Texinfo input format, LaTeX input format, SGML or XML using a publicly available DTD, and standard-conforming simple HTML, PostScript or PDF designed for human modification. Examples of transparent image formats include PNG, XCF and JPG. Opaque formats include proprietary formats that can be read and edited only by proprietary word processors, SGML or XML for which the DTD and/or processing tools are not generally available, and the machine-generated HTML, PostScript or PDF produced by some word processors for output purposes only.

The "Title Page" means, for a printed book, the title page itself, plus such following pages as are needed to hold, legibly, the material this License requires to appear in the title page. For works in formats which do not have any title page as such, "Title Page" means the text near the most prominent appearance of the work's title, preceding the beginning of the body of the text.

A section "Entitled XYZ" means a named subunit of the Document whose title either is precisely XYZ or contains XYZ in parentheses following text that translates XYZ in another language. (Here XYZ stands for a specific section name mentioned below, such as "Acknowledgements", "Dedications", "Endorsements", or "History".) To "Preserve the Title" of such a section when you modify the Document means that it remains a section "Entitled XYZ" according to this definition.

**An American Icon**

The Document may include Warranty Disclaimers next to the notice which states that this License applies to the Document. These Warranty Disclaimers are considered to be included by reference in this License, but only as regards disclaiming warranties: any other implication that these Warranty Disclaimers may have is void and has no effect on the meaning of this License.

## 2. VERBATIM COPYING

You may copy and distribute the Document in any medium, either commercially or noncommercially, provided that this License, the copyright notices, and the license notice saying this License applies to the Document are reproduced in all copies, and that you add no other conditions whatsoever to those of this License. You may not use technical measures to obstruct or control the reading or further copying of the copies you make or distribute. However, you may accept compensation in exchange for copies. If you distribute a large enough number of copies you must also follow the conditions in section 3.

You may also lend copies, under the same conditions stated above, and you may publicly display copies.

## 3. COPYING IN QUANTITY

If you publish printed copies (or copies in media that commonly have printed covers) of the Document, numbering more than 100, and the Document's license notice requires Cover Texts, you must enclose the copies in covers that carry, clearly and legibly, all these Cover Texts: Front-Cover Texts on the front cover, and Back-Cover Texts on the back cover. Both covers must also clearly and legibly identify you as the publisher of these copies. The front cover must present the full title with all words of the title equally prominent and visible. You may add other material on the covers in addition. Copying with changes limited to the covers, as long as they preserve the title of the Document and satisfy these conditions, can be treated as verbatim copying in other respects.

If the required texts for either cover are too voluminous to fit legibly, you should put the first ones listed (as many as fit reasonably) on the actual cover, and continue the rest onto adjacent pages.

**John Wayne**

If you publish or distribute Opaque copies of the Document numbering more than 100, you must either include a machine-readable Transparent copy along with each Opaque copy, or state in or with each Opaque copy a computer-network location from which the general network-using public has access to download using public-standard network protocols a complete Transparent copy of the Document, free of added material. If you use the latter option, you must take reasonably prudent steps, when you begin distribution of Opaque copies in quantity, to ensure that this Transparent copy will remain thus accessible at the stated location until at least one year after the last time you distribute an Opaque copy (directly or through your agents or retailers) of that edition to the public.

It is requested, but not required, that you contact the authors of the Document well before redistributing any large number of copies, to give them a chance to provide you with an updated version of the Document.

## 4. MODIFICATIONS

You may copy and distribute a Modified Version of the Document under the conditions of sections 2 and 3 above, provided that you release the Modified Version under precisely this License, with the Modified Version filling the role of the Document, thus licensing distribution and modification of the Modified Version to whoever possesses a copy of it. In addition, you must do these things in the Modified Version:

* A. Use in the Title Page (and on the covers, if any) a title distinct from that of the Document, and from those of previous versions (which should, if there were any, be listed in the History section of the Document). You may use the same title as a previous version if the original publisher of that version gives permission.
* B. List on the Title Page, as authors, one or more persons or entities responsible for authorship of the modifications in the Modified Version, together with at least five of the principal authors of the Document (all of its principal authors, if it has fewer than five), unless they release you from this requirement.
* C. State on the Title page the name of the publisher of the Modified Version, as the publisher.
* D. Preserve all the copyright notices of the Document.

* E. Add an appropriate copyright notice for your modifications adjacent to the other copyright notices.

* F. Include, immediately after the copyright notices, a license notice giving the public permission to use the Modified Version under the terms of this License, in the form shown in the Addendum below.

* G. Preserve in that license notice the full lists of Invariant Sections and required Cover Texts given in the Document's license notice.

* H. Include an unaltered copy of this License.

* I. Preserve the section Entitled "History", Preserve its Title, and add to it an item stating at least the title, year, new authors, and publisher of the Modified Version as given on the Title Page. If there is no section Entitled "History" in the Document, create one stating the title, year, authors, and publisher of the Document as given on its Title Page, then add an item describing the Modified Version as stated in the previous sentence.

* J. Preserve the network location, if any, given in the Document for public access to a Transparent copy of the Document, and likewise the network locations given in the Document for previous versions it was based on. These may be placed in the "History" section. You may omit a network location for a work that was published at least four years before the Document itself, or if the original publisher of the version it refers to gives permission.

* K. For any section Entitled "Acknowledgements" or "Dedications", Preserve the Title of the section, and preserve in the section all the substance and tone of each of the contributor acknowledgements and/or dedications given therein.

* L. Preserve all the Invariant Sections of the Document, unaltered in their text and in their titles. Section numbers or the equivalent are not considered part of the section titles.

* M. Delete any section Entitled "Endorsements". Such a section may not be included in the Modified Version.

* N. Do not retitle any existing section to be Entitled "Endorsements" or to conflict in title with any Invariant Section.

* O. Preserve any Warranty Disclaimers.

If the Modified Version includes new front-matter sections or appendices that qualify as Secondary Sections and contain no material copied from the Document, you may at your option designate some or all of these sections as invariant. To do this, add their titles to the list of Invariant Sections in the

Modified Version's license notice. These titles must be distinct from any other section titles.

You may add a section Entitled "Endorsements", provided it contains nothing but endorsements of your Modified Version by various parties--for example, statements of peer review or that the text has been approved by an organization as the authoritative definition of a standard.

You may add a passage of up to five words as a Front-Cover Text, and a passage of up to 25 words as a Back-Cover Text, to the end of the list of Cover Texts in the Modified Version. Only one passage of Front-Cover Text and one of Back-Cover Text may be added by (or through arrangements made by) any one entity. If the Document already includes a cover text for the same cover, previously added by you or by arrangement made by the same entity you are acting on behalf of, you may not add another; but you may replace the old one, on explicit permission from the previous publisher that added the old one.

The author(s) and publisher(s) of the Document do not by this License give permission to use their names for publicity for or to assert or imply endorsement of any Modified Version.

## 5. COMBINING DOCUMENTS

You may combine the Document with other documents released under this License, under the terms defined in section 4 above for modified versions, provided that you include in the combination all of the Invariant Sections of all of the original documents, unmodified, and list them all as Invariant Sections of your combined work in its license notice, and that you preserve all their Warranty Disclaimers.

The combined work need only contain one copy of this License, and multiple identical Invariant Sections may be replaced with a single copy. If there are multiple Invariant Sections with the same name but different contents, make the title of each such section unique by adding at the end of it, in parentheses, the name of the original author or publisher of that section if known, or else a unique number. Make the same adjustment to the section titles in the list of Invariant Sections in the license notice of the combined work.

In the combination, you must combine any sections Entitled "History" in the various original documents, forming one section Entitled "History"; likewise combine any sections Entitled "Acknowledgements", and any sections Entitled "Dedications". You must delete all sections Entitled "Endorsements."

## 6. COLLECTIONS OF DOCUMENTS

You may make a collection consisting of the Document and other documents released under this License, and replace the individual copies of this License in the various documents with a single copy that is included in the collection, provided that you follow the rules of this License for verbatim copying of each of the documents in all other respects.

You may extract a single document from such a collection, and distribute it individually under this License, provided you insert a copy of this License into the extracted document, and follow this License in all other respects regarding verbatim copying of that document.

## 7. AGGREGATION WITH INDEPENDENT WORKS

A compilation of the Document or its derivatives with other separate and independent documents or works, in or on a volume of a storage or distribution medium, is called an "aggregate" if the copyright resulting from the compilation is not used to limit the legal rights of the compilation's users beyond what the individual works permit. When the Document is included in an aggregate, this License does not apply to the other works in the aggregate which are not themselves derivative works of the Document.

If the Cover Text requirement of section 3 is applicable to these copies of the Document, then if the Document is less than one half of the entire aggregate, the Document's Cover Texts may be placed on covers that bracket the Document within the aggregate, or the electronic equivalent of covers if the Document is in electronic form. Otherwise they must appear on printed covers that bracket the whole aggregate.

**John Wayne**

## 8. TRANSLATION

Translation is considered a kind of modification, so you may distribute
translations of the Document under the terms of section 4. Replacing
Invariant Sections with translations requires special permission from their
copyright holders, but you may include translations of some or all Invariant
Sections in addition to the original versions of these Invariant Sections. You
may include a translation of this License, and all the license notices in the
Document, and any Warranty Disclaimers, provided that you also include
the original English version of this License and the original versions of
those notices and disclaimers. In case of a disagreement between the
translation and the original version of this License or a notice or disclaimer,
the original version will prevail.

If a section in the Document is Entitled "Acknowledgements",
"Dedications", or "History", the requirement (section 4) to Preserve its Title
(section 1) will typically require changing the actual title.

## 9. TERMINATION

You may not copy, modify, sublicense, or distribute the Document except
as expressly provided for under this License. Any other attempt to copy,
modify, sublicense or distribute the Document is void, and will
automatically terminate your rights under this License. However, parties
who have received copies, or rights, from you under this License will not
have their licenses terminated so long as such parties remain in full
compliance.

## 10. FUTURE REVISIONS OF THIS LICENSE

The Free Software Foundation may publish new, revised versions of the
GNU Free Documentation License from time to time. Such new versions
will be similar in spirit to the present version, but may differ in detail to
address new problems or concerns. See http://www.gnu.org/copyleft/.

Each version of the License is given a distinguishing version number. If the
Document specifies that a particular numbered version of this License "or
any later version" applies to it, you have the option of following the terms

and conditions either of that specified version or of any later version that has been published (not as a draft) by the Free Software Foundation. If the Document does not specify a version number of this License, you may choose any version ever published (not as a draft) by the Free Software Foundation.

How to use this License for your documents

To use this License in a document you have written, include a copy of the License in the document and put the following copyright and license notices just after the title page:

Copyright (c) YEAR YOUR NAME.
Permission is granted to copy, distribute and/or modify this document under the terms of the GNU Free Documentation License, Version 1.2 or any later version published by the Free Software Foundation; with no Invariant Sections, no Front-Cover Texts, and no Back-Cover Texts. A copy of the license is included in the section entitled "GNU
Free Documentation License".

If you have Invariant Sections, Front-Cover Texts and Back-Cover Texts, replace the "with...Texts." line with this:

with the Invariant Sections being LIST THEIR TITLES, with the Front-Cover Texts being LIST, and with the Back-Cover Texts being LIST.

If you have Invariant Sections without Cover Texts, or some other combination of the three, merge those two alternatives to suit the situation.

If your document contains nontrivial examples of program code, we recommend releasing these examples in parallel under your choice of free software license, such as the GNU General Public License, to permit their use in free software.

Breinigsville, PA USA
08 December 2010
250913BV00006B/64/P